THIS JOURNAL BEL

Grandma   Grandson

Name: Name:

....

We start this journey with:

....

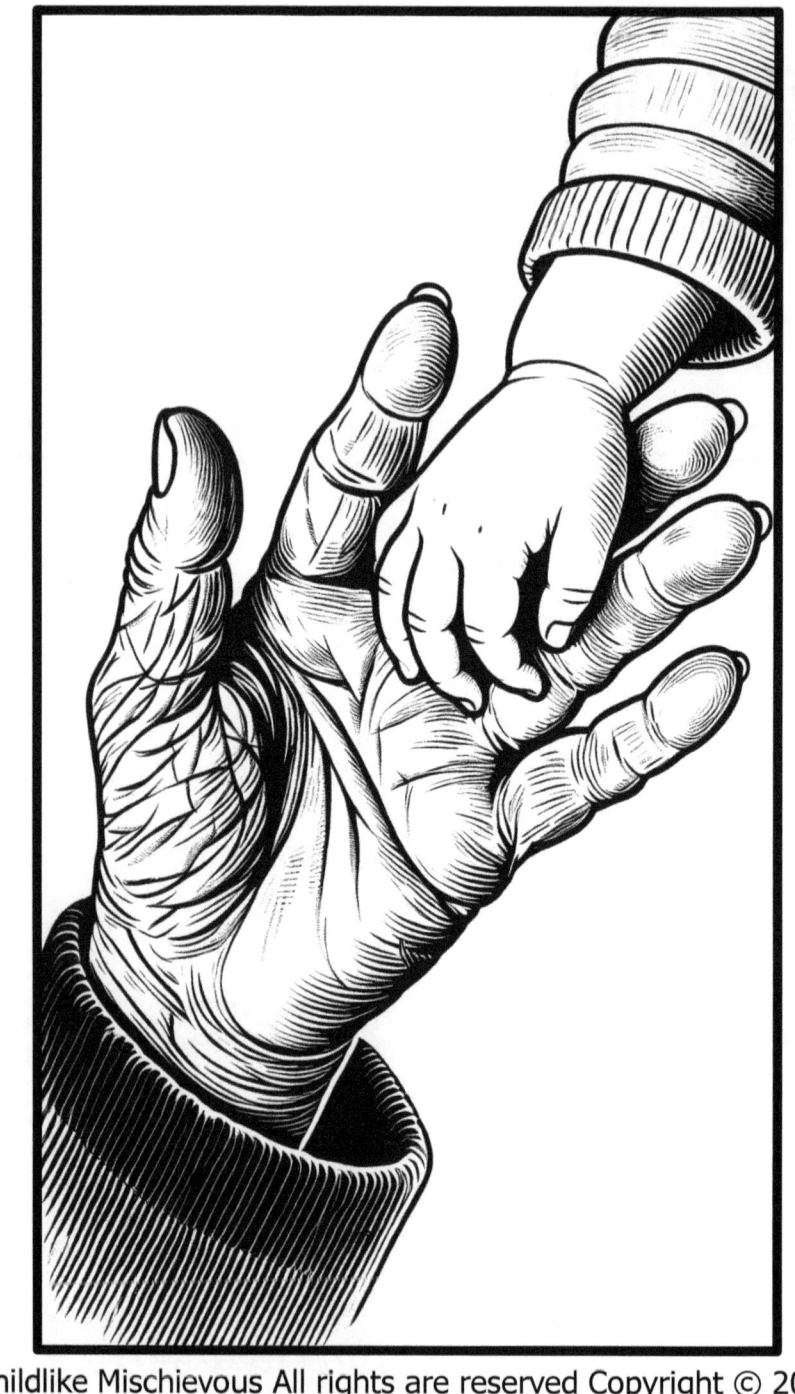

Childlike Mischievous All rights are reserved Copyright © 2024
No part of this publication may be reproduced, stored in a retrieval system, or transmitted in any form or by any means, electronic, mechanical, photocopying, recording, or otherwise, without prior permission.

Today marks the beginning of a special journey together – a journey of discovery, connection, and meaningful conversations through this journal. This is more than just a place for words; it's a space where you can share your thoughts, dreams, and moments that bring you closer as Grandmother and Grandson. As you fill these pages, remember that every entry is a step toward understanding each other more deeply and creating memories that will last a lifetime. Here's to the start of something truly amazing – your shared story.

About Grandma

Name: _____

Age: _____

Hair Color: _____

Eye Color: _____

Height: _____

Favorite Color: _____

Favorite Animal: _____

A list of names my Grandson uses to refer to me:

_____

_____

_____

About Grandma

Here is a list of words I would use to describe my Grandma:

_____

_____

_____

Here is list of things she says all the time:

_____

_____

_____

_____

About Me

Name: _____

Age: _____

Hair Color: _____

Eye Color: _____

Height: _____

Favorite Color: _____

Favorite Animal: _____

A list of names Grandma uses for me:

_____

_____

_____

About Me

Grandma, list the words you would use to describe me:

_____

_____

_____

_____

List the things I say all the time:

_____

_____

_____

_____

_____

Grandma and Me

Attach photo of Grandma & Me

Grandma and Me

Here is a silly song we wrote:

Grandma

What was your day like when you were my age?

_____

_____

_____

_____

What was your favorite food when you were a child?

_____

_____

_____

_____

Grandson

What is your favorite food?

_____

_____

_____

_____

What makes you feel happy and calm when you're by yourself?

_____

_____

_____

Grandma

Do you remember your first school? What memories do you have from it?

_____
_____
_____
_____

What toys did you like to play with when you were little?

_____
_____
_____
_____

Grandson

What makes you feel proud of yourself?

_____

_____

_____

_____

What do you enjoy doing in your free time?

_____

_____

_____

_____

Grandma

Did you have any pets when you were young? What kind of animals were they?

_____

_____

_____

_____

What were your dreams when you were my age?

_____

_____

_____

_____

Grandson

Do you have a favorite toy? What is it?

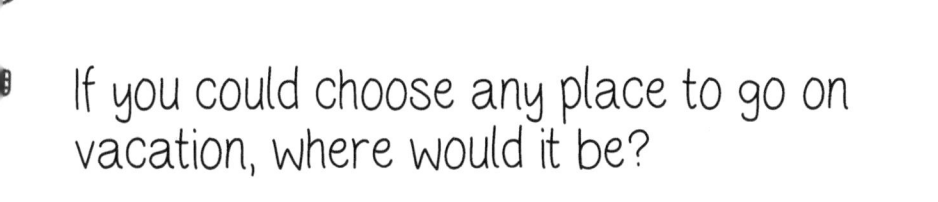

_____
_____
_____
_____

If you could choose any place to go on vacation, where would it be?

_____
_____
_____
_____

Grandma

What were your favorite games to play with friends?

_____

_____

_____

_____

Did you ever go on a special vacation? Where was it?

_____

_____

_____

_____

Grandson

What is your favorite holiday and why?

_____
_____
_____
_____

What do you want to be when you grow up?

_____
_____
_____
_____

Grandma

What was your favorite holiday when you were a child?

_____

_____

_____

_____

Did you have any chores to do at home when you were little?

_____

_____

_____

_____

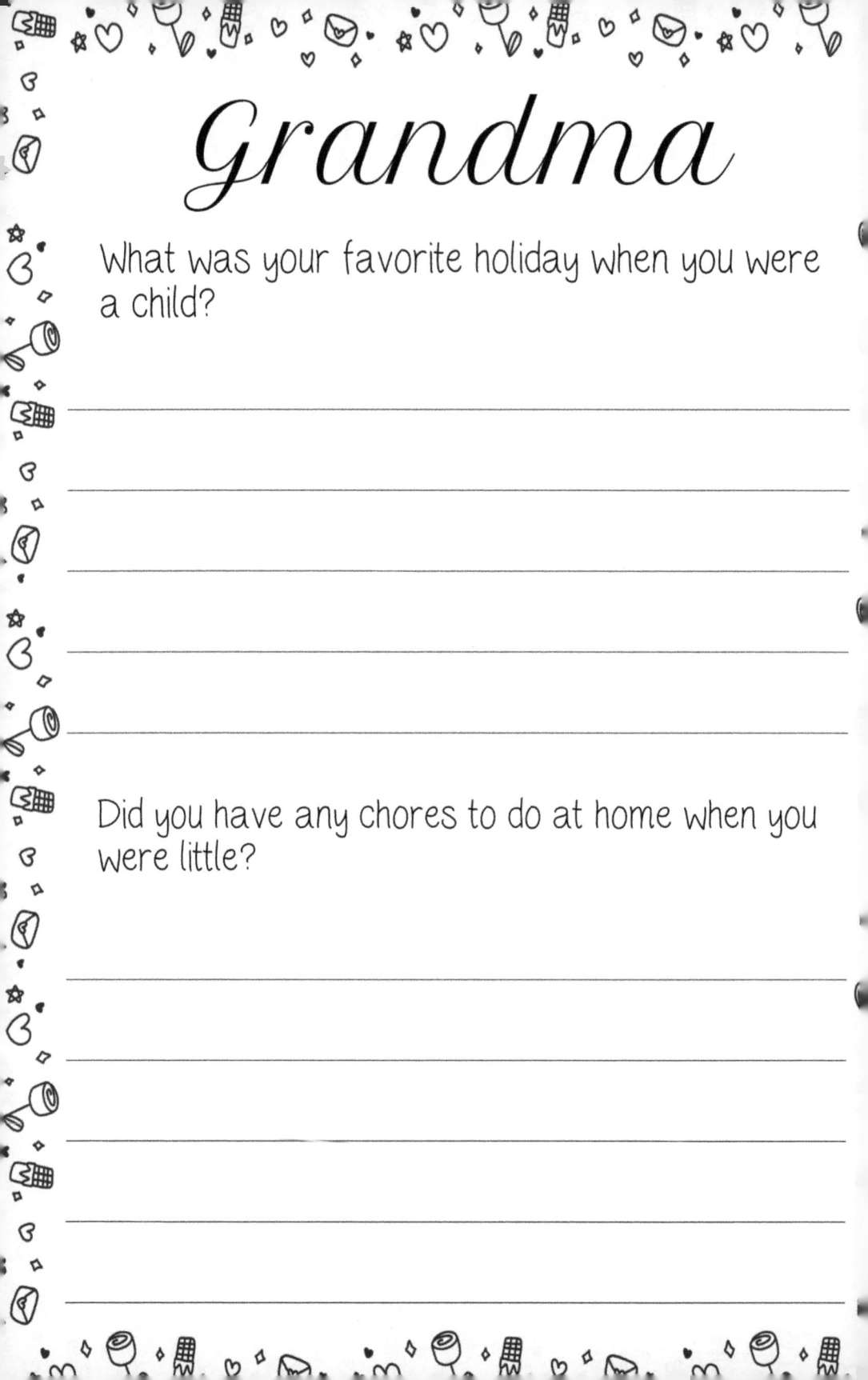

Grandson

Do you have a favorite character from a cartoon or book? Who is it?

_____

_____

_____

_____

Do you have any hobbies you'd like to tell me about?

_____

_____

_____

_____

Grandma

The time and place I was born is...

_____

_____

My most memorable birthday is...

_____

_____

My favorite ever present was...

_____

_____

Grandson

The time and place I was born is...

_____

_____

My most memorable birthday is...

_____

_____

My favorite ever present was...

_____

_____

Grandma

What do you think makes you such a warm and wise person?

1

_____

_____

2

_____

_____

3

_____

_____

Grandson

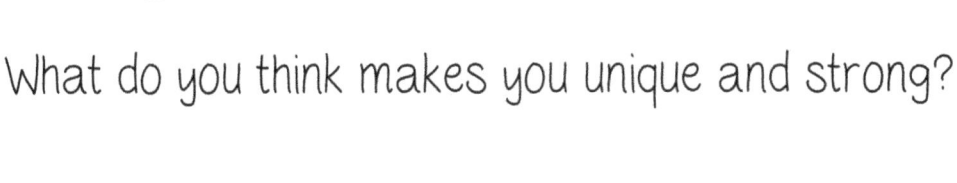

What do you think makes you unique and strong?

1
_____

_____

2
_____

_____

3
_____

_____

Grandma

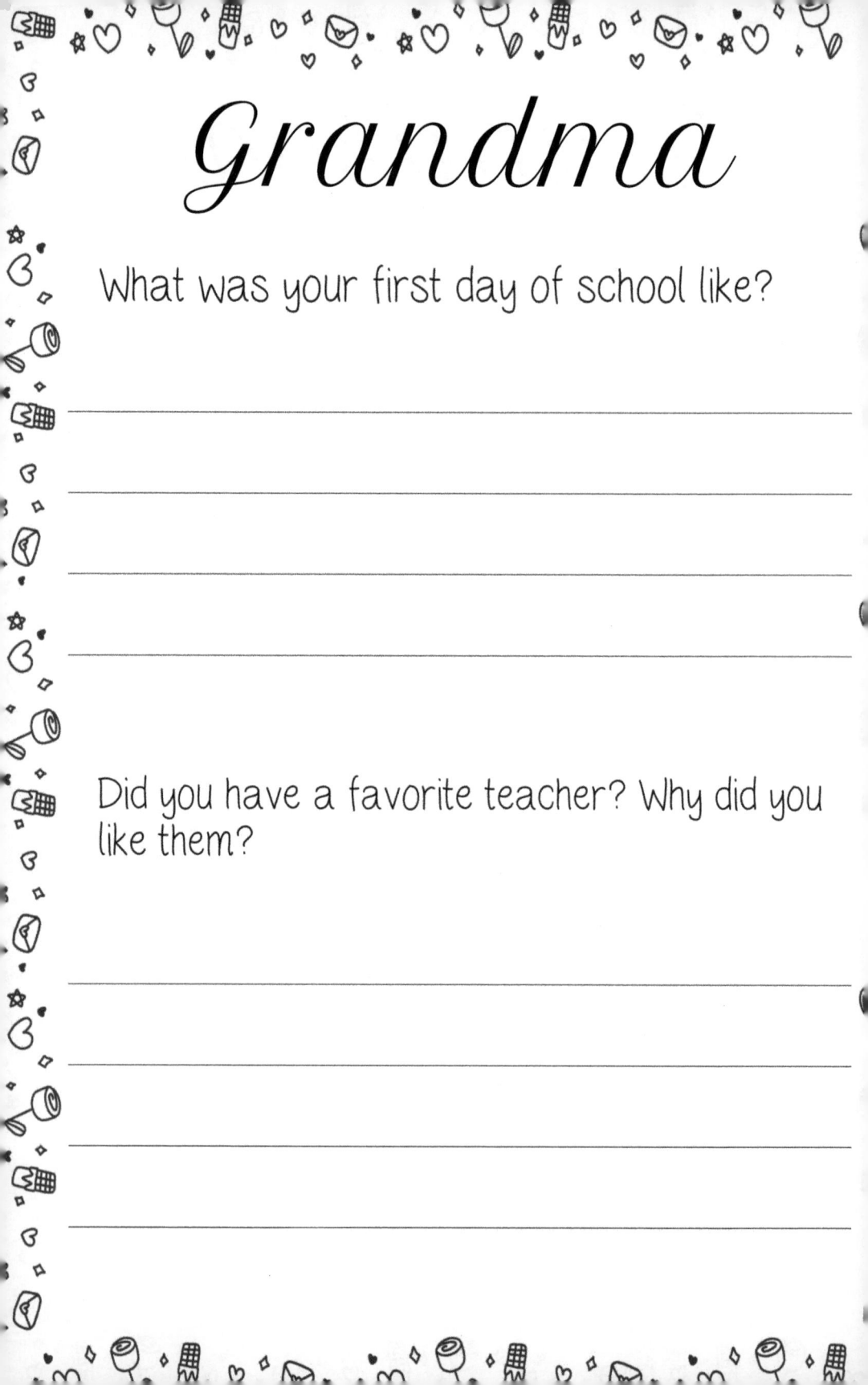

What was your first day of school like?

_____
_____
_____

Did you have a favorite teacher? Why did you like them?

_____
_____
_____

Grandson

What makes you feel happy?

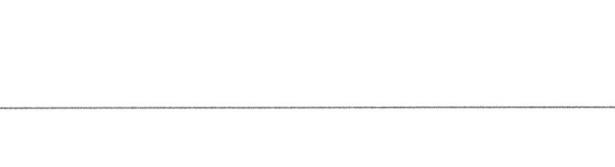

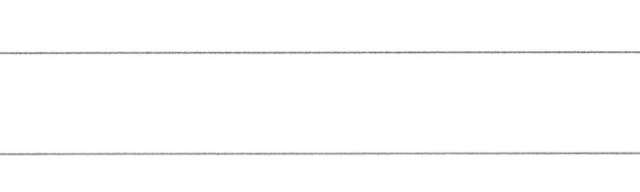

_____

_____

_____

What is your favorite animal and why?

_____

_____

_____

Grandma

Did you have a best friend? What was their name?

_____

_____

_____

_____

What made you laugh a lot when you were a child?

_____

_____

_____

_____

Grandson

If you could have a superpower, what would it be?

_____

_____

_____

_____

What do you like to do with your friends the most?

_____

_____

_____

_____

Grandma

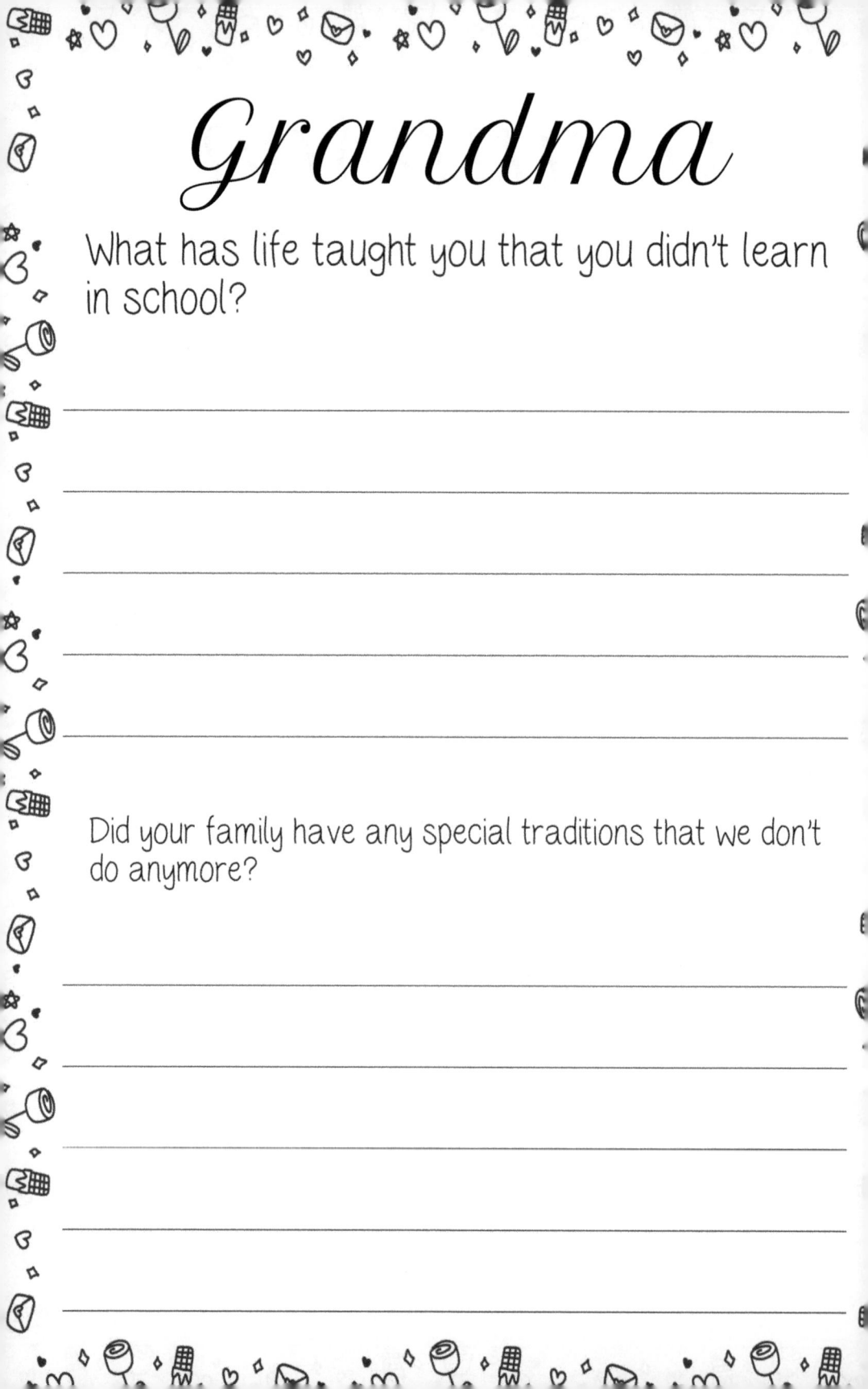

What has life taught you that you didn't learn in school?

_____
_____
_____
_____

Did your family have any special traditions that we don't do anymore?

_____
_____
_____
_____
_____

Grandson

Is there something you'd like to learn or try?

_____

_____

_____

_____

What is your favorite family vacation memory?

_____

_____

_____

_____

Grandma

What makes you feel happiest in life?

_____

_____

_____

_____

Was there something that worried you when you were my age?

_____

_____

_____

_____

Grandson

What makes you happiest in your everyday life?

_____

_____

_____

_____

Has anything worried you recently?

_____

_____

_____

_____

Grandma

What dream have you fulfilled, and what dream do you still have?

_____

_____

_____

_____

Was there a moment in your life that made you feel especially happy?

_____

_____

_____

_____

Grandson

What are your dreams for the future?

_____
_____
_____
_____

Do you have a memory that always makes you smile?

_____
_____
_____
_____

Family Photos

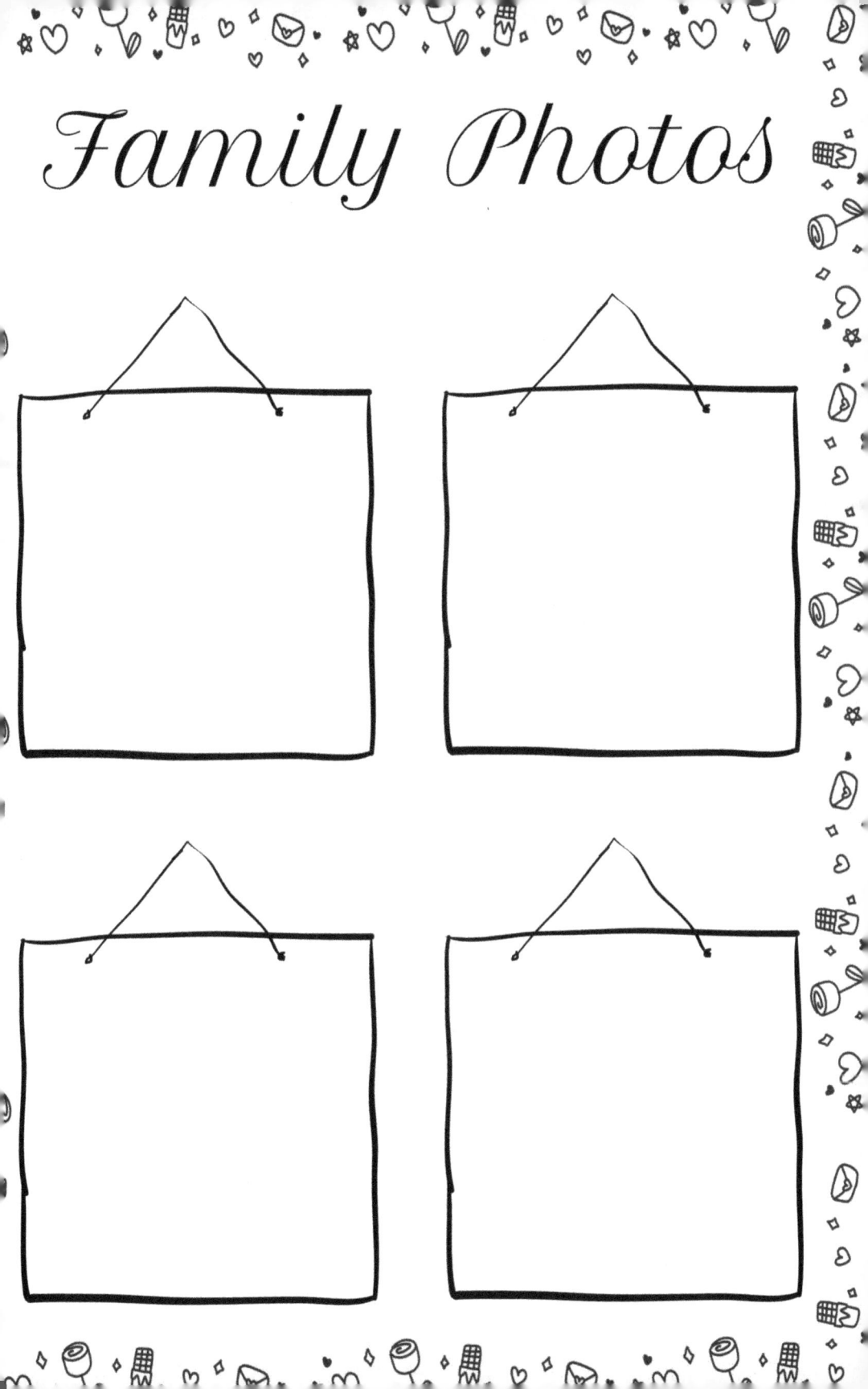

Family Photos

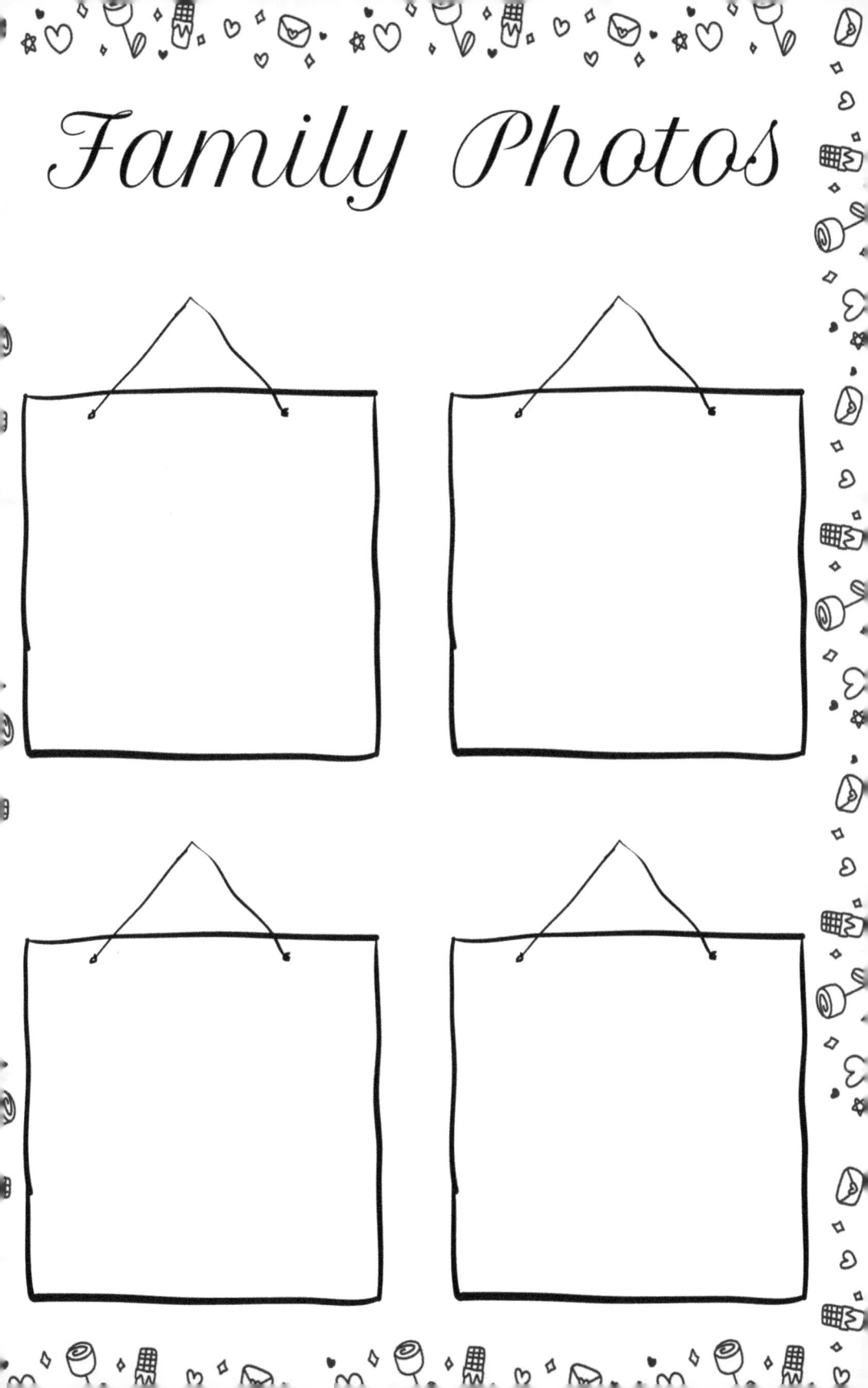

Grandma

What is it about you that always makes me feel loved and safe?

Grandson

What do you do that always makes me proud of you?

Grandma

If I could have three wishes, they would be...

1

_____

_____

2

_____

_____

3

_____

_____

Grandson

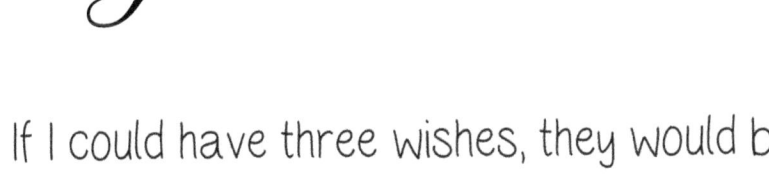

If I could have three wishes, they would be...

1

_____

_____

2

_____

_____

3

_____

_____

Grandma

How did you deal with difficult times when you were younger?

_____

_____

_____

_____

Did you ever have a dream that seemed impossible but came true?

_____

_____

_____

_____

Grandson

What do you do when you feel sad or worried?

_____
_____
_____
_____

Is there something you dream about, but it feels very hard to achieve?

_____
_____
_____
_____

Grandma

What do you think makes our relationship so strong?

1

_____

_____

2

_____

_____

3

_____

_____

Grandson

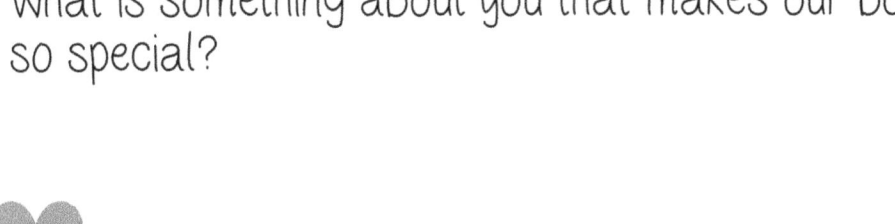

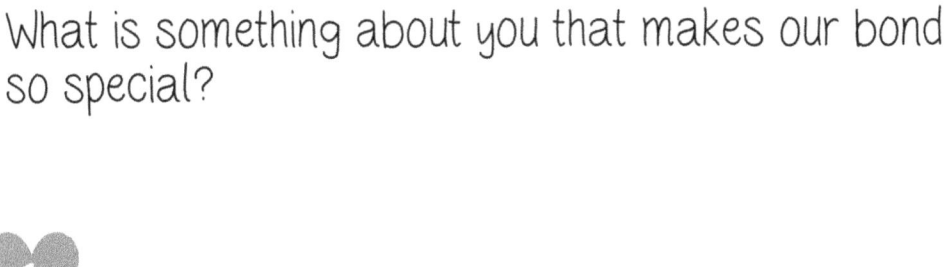

What is something about you that makes our bond so special?

1

_____

_____

2

_____

_____

3

_____

_____

Grandma

If I could imagine myself wearing an amazing outfit that would make me feel more confident when I'm anxious, it would look like this...

Grandson

Grandson.. When you feel anxious or lack confidence, imagine yourself wearing an amazing outfit. Everyone thinks you look wonderful. Draw a picture and describe what it looks like...

_____

_____

Grandma

What always calms you down when you feel worried?

_____

_____

_____

_____

What childhood memory makes you laugh the most?

_____

_____

_____

_____

Grandson

What helps you feel better when you have a tough day?

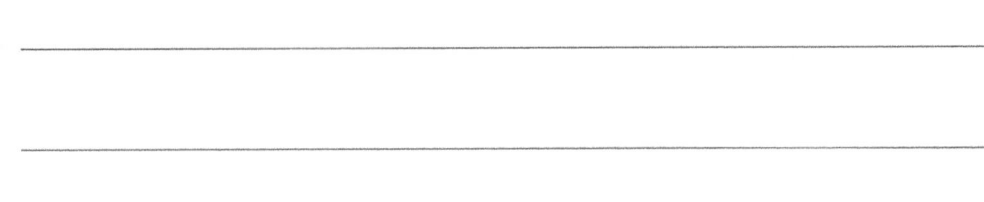

_____

_____

_____

_____

What is your most beautiful memory from a vacation or family gathering?

_____

_____

_____

_____

Grandma

Grandma, tell me about the strangest dream you ever had...

_____
_____
_____
_____
_____
_____
_____
_____
_____
_____
_____
_____
_____
_____

Grandson

Grandson, tell me about the strangest dream you've ever had...

___
___
___
___
___
___
___
___
___
___
___

Grandma

Did you ever have a dream at night that meant something special to you?

_____

_____

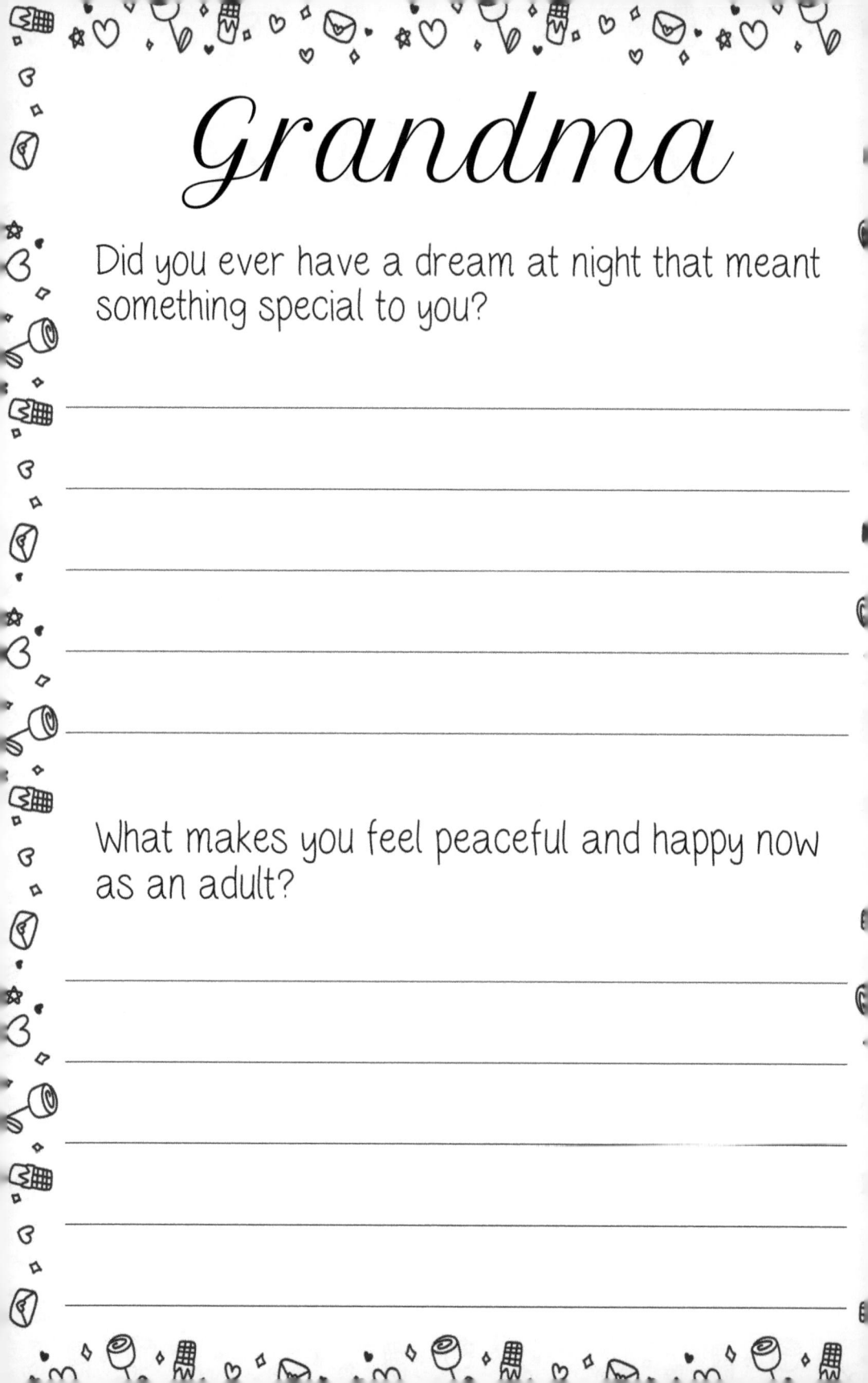

_____

_____

What makes you feel peaceful and happy now as an adult?

_____

_____

_____

_____

Grandson

What do you often dream about when you fall asleep?

_____

_____

_____

_____

What makes you feel happy when you're with your family?

_____

_____

_____

_____

Grandma

This is Grandma, he looks happy...

This is Grandma being silly

Grandson

Grandson, this is you looking happy...

Grandson, this is you being silly...

Grandma

If I could have three superpowers, they would be...

1

_____
_____

2

_____
_____

3

_____
_____

Grandson

If I could have three superpowers, they would be...

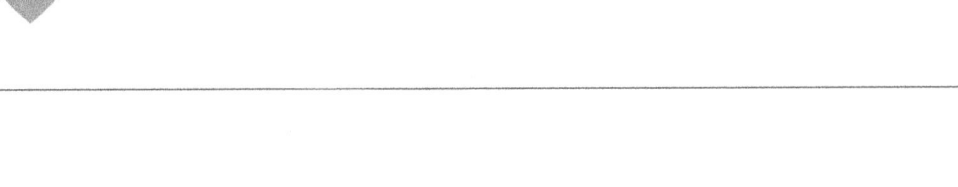

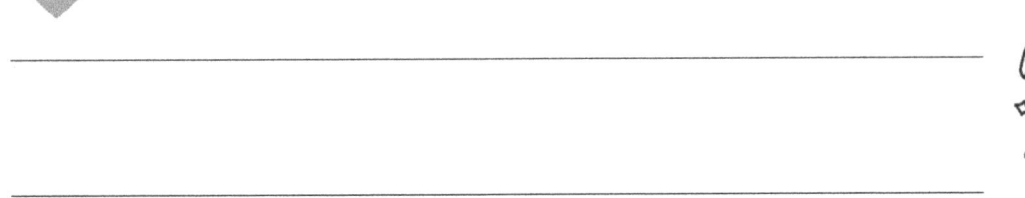

1

_____

_____

2

_____

_____

3

_____

_____

Grandma

My best friends as a child were...

_____

_____

My best friends now are...

_____

_____

What I've learned about friendships are...

_____

_____

Grandson

My best friends are...

_____

_____

_____

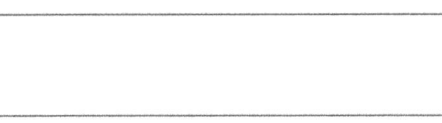

The things I like best about my friends are...

_____

_____

_____

The things I don't like about my friends are...

_____

_____

_____

Grandma

Grandma, did you sleep with a cuddly toy when you were young?
Tell me about it?

_____
_____
_____
_____
_____
_____
_____
_____
_____
_____
_____

Grandson

My favorite cuddly toy is a _____ called _____.
I will never throw it away because...

_____

_____

_____

_____

_____

_____

_____

_____

Grandma

Was there a person in your life who helped you get through tough times?

_____

_____

_____

_____

What made you feel safe when you were a child?

_____

_____

_____

_____

Grandson

Is there someone who always knows how to cheer you up?

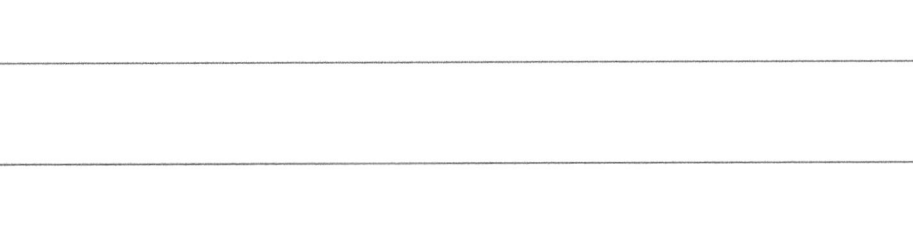

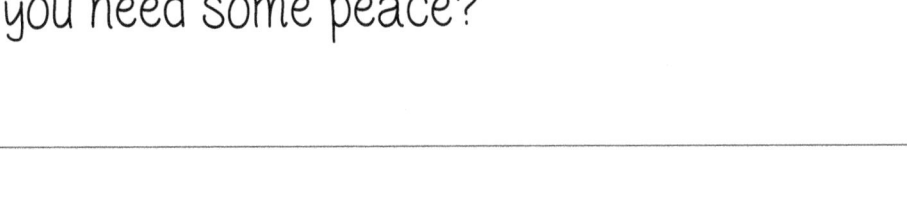

_____

_____

_____

_____

What is your favorite place to relax when you need some peace?

_____

_____

_____

_____

Grandma

Tunes

My top 10 songs of all time are...

1. _____
2. _____
3. _____
4. _____
5. _____
6. _____
7. _____
8. _____
9. _____
10. _____

Grandson

Tunes

My favourite top 10 songs are...

1. _____
2. _____
3. _____
4. _____
5. _____
6. _____
7. _____
8. _____
9. _____
10. _____

Grandma

Grandma, tell me about something kind you did for someone...

Grandson

Grandson, tell me about something kind you did for someone...

_____
_____
_____
_____
_____
_____
_____
_____
_____
_____
_____
_____
_____

Grandma

What place is the most happy or calming for you?

_____
_____
_____
_____

What would you like me to remember about you when I grow up?

_____
_____
_____
_____

Grandson

What is the biggest dream you've had for as long as you can remember?

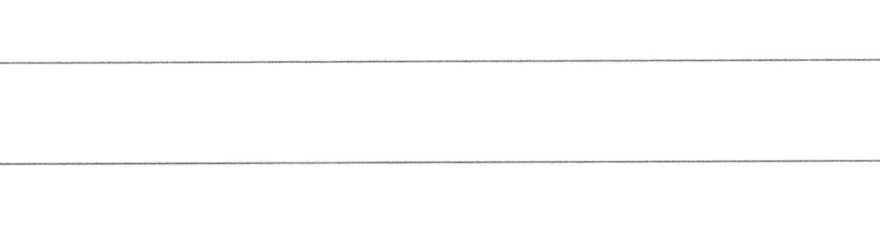

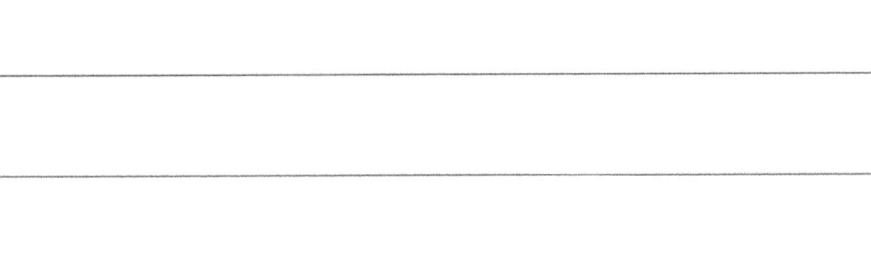

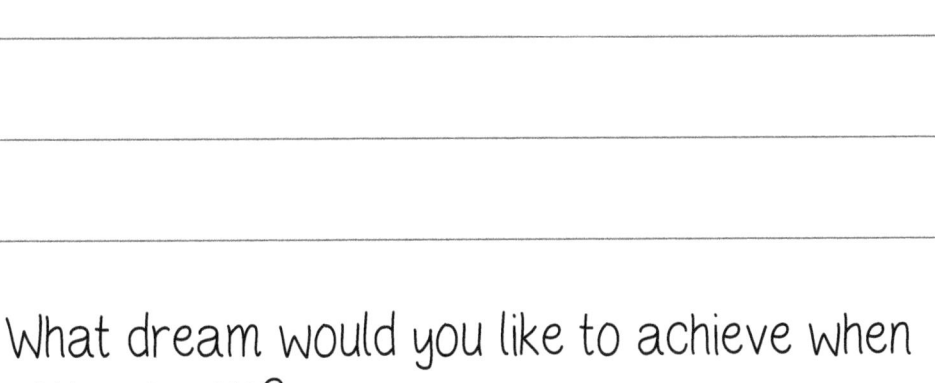

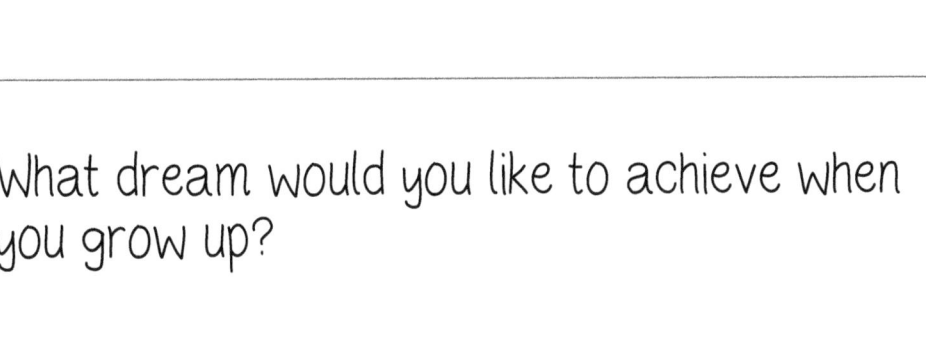

_____

_____

_____

_____

What dream would you like to achieve when you grow up?

_____

_____

_____

_____

Grandma

If you could have dinner with anyone in the world - past or present - who would it be and why?

Grandson

If you could spend a whole day doing anything you want, what would your perfect day look like?

_____

_____

_____

_____

_____

_____

_____

_____

_____

Grandma

The person I went to with my worries when I was young was...

_____

_____

_____

If I ever want to talk about my feelings, I solemnly swear to talk to you or...

_____

_____

_____

Signature: _____

Grandson

The person I will go to with my worries will be...

_____

_____

_____

If I ever want to talk about my feelings,
I solemnly swear that I will talk to you or...

_____

_____

_____

Signature: _____

Grandma

Other Things I Want To Say To You,

_____
_____
_____
_____
_____
_____
_____
_____
_____
_____
_____

Grandson

Other Things I Want To Say To You,

Grandma

Other Things I Want To Say To You,

_____
_____
_____
_____
_____
_____
_____
_____
_____
_____
_____
_____

Grandson

Other Things I Want To Say To You,

_____

_____

_____

_____

_____

_____

_____

_____

_____

_____

Dear Grandma and Beloved Grandson,

As you reach the end of this shared journey through the pages of this journal, I want you both to remember the special time you spent together. Every conversation, question, and answer has built a foundation of love, mutual respect, and understanding between you. The memories you've shared here are not only a record of your history but also a testament to the incredible bond you have, growing stronger with each passing day.

Grandma, your wisdom and life experiences are invaluable. By sharing them, you have given your grandson a treasure that will stay with him forever. Your stories, advice, and love will accompany him through every stage of life. Your words are not just memories from the past but also guiding lights for the future.

Grandson, your questions and curiosity show how much you want to know and understand your grandmother, and how deeply you value her presence in your life. Every conversation has been an opportunity to grow closer, to build memories together that will become a precious legacy for years to come.

Let this journal be a reminder of the importance of family bonds, of nurturing closeness, and of continually discovering new sides of each other. May your conversations never end, and may the love you've written down here be seen every day in your gestures, words, and shared moments. What you have created will endure for generations and become a cherished keepsake for you and your family.

We hope this journal marks the beginning of even more shared moments and conversations that will last a lifetime. The memories you have captured here will always be with you, and each new conversation will fill your hearts with joy and love.

Milton Keynes UK
Ingram Content Group UK Ltd.
UKHW020117221024
449869UK00011B/505

9 788368 294149